MY FIRST
GUITAR

Learn To Play
Right Away!

Ben Parker

Author: Ben Parker

Editor: Alison McNicol

First published in 2013 by Kyle Craig Publishing

This version updated June 2017

Text and illustration copyright © 2013 Kyle Craig Publishing

Design and illustration: Julie Anson

Music set by Ben Parker using Sibelius software

ISBN: 978-1-908707-13-0

A CIP record for this book is available from the British Library.

A Kyle Craig Publication
www.kyle-craig.com

Contents

Welcome To Your 'My First Guitar Book'!

The guitar is such a fun instrument to learn and play, and I hope that with the help of this book you will have a blast learning lots of new guitar skills!

This book is full of fun limericks and well known songs, and will give you a great introduction to the guitar and have you playing and singing along in no time!

Like any new skill, it takes a little time before you get the hang of things.

The more you practice playing your guitar, the easier it will become and the better you will be.

Why not aim to practice at least 10 minutes every day...then you'll be able to play all the way to the end of this book in no time at all!

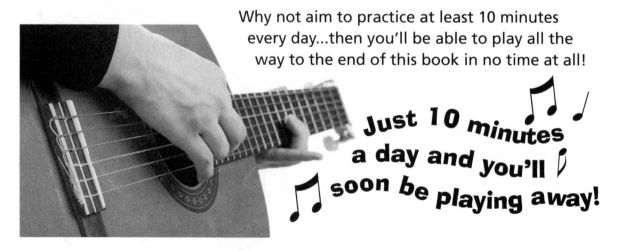

Just 10 minutes a day and you'll soon be playing away!

 # About The Guitar

The first guitar-like instruments were made and played in Europe in the 1100's. The six-stringed, curved bodied guitar as we know it today was developed in the 1400s in Spain.

The guitar comes in many types, shapes and sizes. The most popular types of guitar used today are **steel string acoustic guitars** and **electric guitars** although beginners often begin by playing a nylon string (or Classical) guitar.

 # The Instrument

ACOUSTIC

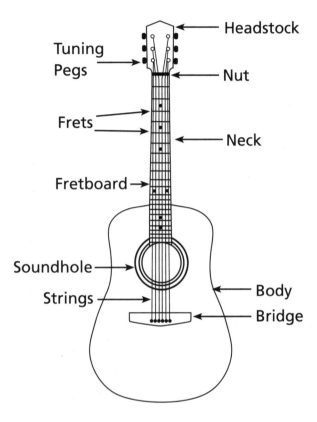

Tuning Pegs
Frets
Fretboard →
Soundhole →
Strings →

Headstock
Nut
Neck
Body
Bridge

ELECTRIC

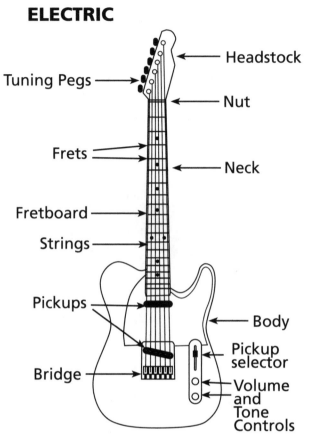

Tuning Pegs →
Frets
Fretboard →
Strings →
Pickups →
Bridge →

Headstock
Nut
Neck
Body
Pickup selector
Volume and Tone Controls

 # How To Hold The Guitar

You can play the guitar whilst standing up (using a strap) or sitting down. Your right arm should hang down and over the guitar as shown.

What To Do With Your Hands

LEFT HAND POSITION

Your left hand position is really important. Make sure your thumb is around the back of the neck. When you fret a note it should be like 'pinching' the neck between your thumb and forefinger. Fretting will be explained in more detail later on in the book.

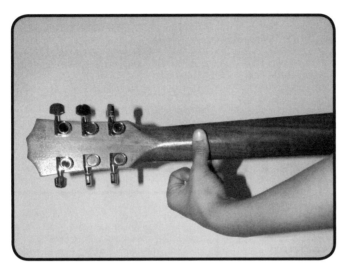

RIGHT HAND POSITION

When seated, let the curve of the guitar's body sit on your right leg. Try to keep this leg upright to stop your guitar slipping downwards. When using a strap in standing position, let the guitar hang off your shoulder. It should sit snuggly between your right forearm and your body.

LEFT HANDED PLAYERS

Some left handed players play the guitar right-handed (with the headstock pointing to the left). If you are left-handed try playing in the right hand position shown and see how it feels. If it feels strange, try playing it the other way round (with the guitar headstock pointing to your right). If this feels more comfortable then you'll need to have the guitar re-strung upside down. Ask at your local music store — they should be able to do this for you.

Using A Plectrum/Pick

You can use your right hand fingers to play the guitar but many players use a **plectrum** (often called a **pick**) to strum chords and pick single notes. It is best to strum across the soundhole of the guitar. If strumming with your fingers (without a pick) use your thumb to strum downwards and your fingers for the upstroke.

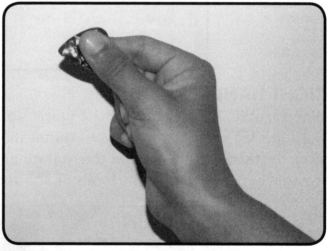

Picks come in different thicknesses. A medium pick (nylon.60mm) is probably the best one to start with.

 # Tuning

The strings of the guitar are tuned to the notes **E, A, D, G, B** and **E**. These strings are known as the 'open' strings. Pressing down on a string with a left hand finger to change the pitch of the note is called fretting.

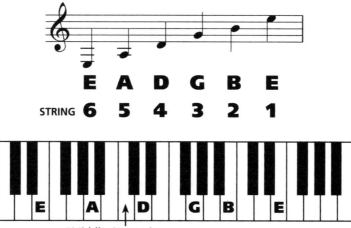

To keep your guitar in tune you can use a piano to help you find the notes or you can use one of the many digital tuning apps now available for smartphones and laptops. There are also certain websites which give you a 'player' which allows you to play recorded guitar notes as a reference.

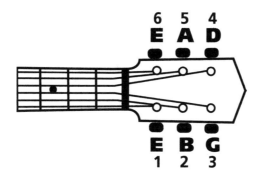

TUNING PEGS	To Make Your Note Lower	To Make Your Note Higher
TURN PEGS ON TOP ROW (E, A & D strings)	**CLOCKWISE**	**ANTI-CLOCKWISE**
TURN PEGS ON BOTTOM ROW (G,B & E strings)	**ANTI-CLOCKWISE**	**CLOCKWISE**

Chords and Strumming

Chords are made up of two or more notes played together at the same time. Earlier we told you about your right hand and holding a pick and now we'll show you how strumming works.

To start with we'll just use the open strings to practice this. This means you don't have to push any strings down with your left hand fingers. You may need to hold the neck of your guitar, without touching any strings, to keep it steady whilst you do this.

First of all bring your right hand up above the strings holding your thumb (or pick) out.

STRUM!

Then bring your hand down and use your thumb (or pick) to stroke across the strings.

Follow the strum through until you've played across all six strings.

How To Read Chord Diagrams

Now we'll try playing chords, which means using our left hand as well as our right. To do this you will need to fret the notes of the chord. This means you'll use the fingers of your left hand to push down on one or more string.

Chords are played using 'shapes' which are written using chord diagrams. Chord diagrams are simple box diagrams for each chord, showing you where to put your left hand fingers on the frets.

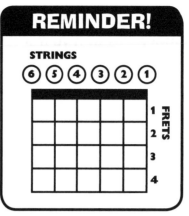

REMINDER!

STRINGS

⑥ ⑤ ④ ③ ② ①

FRETS 1 2 3 4

The numbers above the box diagram show you what left hand finger to use to press down/fret with. These are called fingerings.

If the fingering reads **0** it means you let the string ring **open** (don't fret this string).

So, for the **G** chord we need to use our **3rd finger** on our left hand, to push down on the **3rd fret** on the top (**E**) string. Where you see an **X** symbol, this means **don't** play that string.

All the chords in this book are played on the **top FOUR strings only**

Example: G Chord

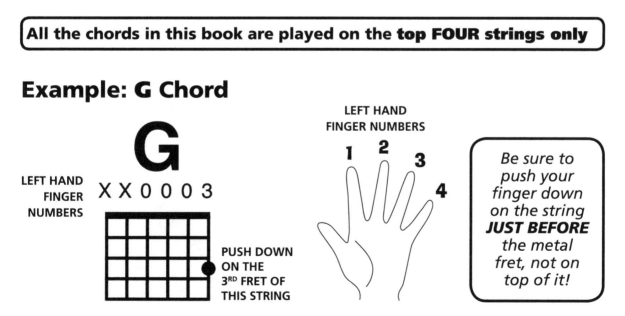

G

LEFT HAND FINGER NUMBERS

X X 0 0 0 3

PUSH DOWN ON THE 3RD FRET OF THIS STRING

LEFT HAND FINGER NUMBERS

1 2 3 4

Be sure to push your finger down on the string *JUST BEFORE* the metal fret, not on top of it!

# The Chord Of G

This is nice and easy because you only need to push down with one left hand finger. Position your left hand thumb behind the neck as shown on page 7, and push down on your (top) **E** string with your **3rd finger** on the **3rd fret**.

Limericks and rhymes are always a fun way to practice your chords and make people laugh at the same time!

Strum a downstroke on your **G** chord whenever you see a word in BOLD. The chord name will be written above too to remind you. Make sure you only strum the **TOP FOUR STRINGS** (**D, G, B** & **E**) — the **X** symbol means don't play that string.

G   G
When I **take** my guitar from its **case**

G   G
A big **smile** you will see on my **face**

G
To **learn** is such fun

G
And I've **only** begun

G   G
Now I'm **playing** all over the **place**!

The Chord Of C

Time to learn a new chord!

Let's do **C** next.

You'll need two fingers to push down for this one.

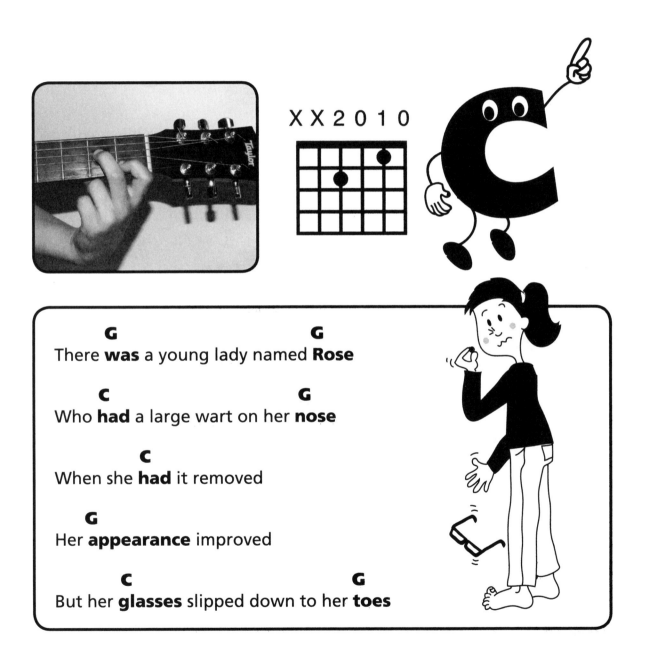

XX 2 0 1 0

    G   G
There **was** a young lady named **Rose**

      C   G
Who **had** a large wart on her **nose**

         C
When she **had** it removed

   G
Her **appearance** improved

      C   G
But her **glasses** slipped down to her **toes**

The Chord Of D7

Now let's learn our third chord — **D7**.

 X X 0 2 1 3

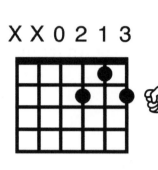

This last limerick has all three chords in. Take it slowly at first until you get used to the changes between chords.

     G   **G**
There **was** an Old Man in a **tree**

     C   **G**
Who was **horribly** bugged by a **bee**;

     C
When they **said**, "Does it buzz?"

     G
He re-**plied**, "Yes, it does!"

     D7   **G**
"And it's **currently** stinging my **knee**"

CHORD REMINDER!

G	**C**	**D7**
X X 0 0 0 3	X X 2 0 1 0	X X 0 2 1 3

The Chord Of E Minor

Try playing your new **E minor** chord below — it's written down as **Em** — the little **m** stands for **minor**! Have a listen to the chord, some people think Minor chords sound sad...what do you think?

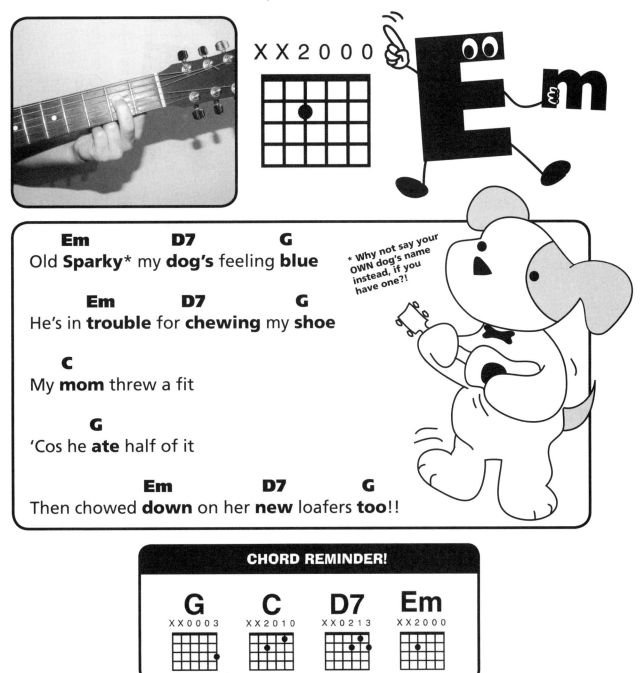

XX 2 0 0 0

Em   D7   G
Old **Sparky*** my **dog's** feeling **blue**

* Why not say your OWN dog's name instead, if you have one?!

Em   D7   G
He's in **trouble** for **chewing** my **shoe**

C
My **mom** threw a fit

G
'Cos he **ate** half of it

Em   D7   G
Then chowed **down** on her **new** loafers **too**!!

CHORD REMINDER!

G   C   D7   Em
XX0003   XX2010   XX0213   XX2000

15

Strumming Patterns

When you use a mixture of down strokes and up strokes it is called a strumming pattern. Let's try a simple one first:

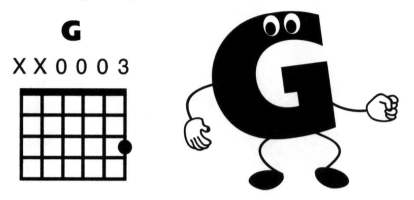

G

X X 0 0 0 3

Hold down a **G** chord and try playing 4 down strokes as shown below.

Count 1, 2, 3, 4 as you strum *downwards*.

↓ ↓ ↓ ↓

1 2 3 4

Now try an *upstroke*. Use the index or 1st finger of your right hand (or pick if you use one) for this and brush upwards across the strings.

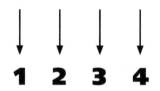

↑

1

Now try going between the *down-stroke* and the *up-stroke*. Still counting but saying '*and*' on the upstroke at the end of the pattern.

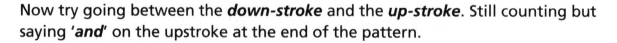

↓ ↓ ↓ ↓ ↑

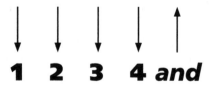

1   2   3   4 *and*

Now try an *upstroke after* every *downstroke*:

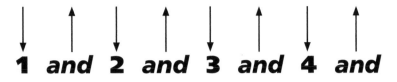

1 and 2 and 3 and 4 and

Now you're ready to try playing through a proper song. This first verse of **'Wheels On The Bus'** is written in musical form using bars (or measures).

First let's try a simple strumming pattern, using only a *DOWN* stroke and just 2 chords — **G** and **D7**.

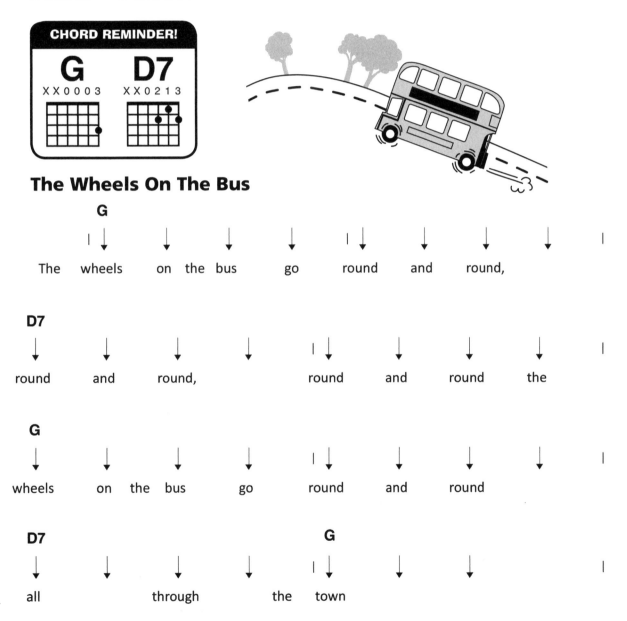

The Wheels On The Bus

	G						
The	wheels	on	the	bus	go	round	and	round,

D7

round and round, round and round the

G

wheels on the bus go round and round

D7 ... G

all through the town

Now let's try the song again, using **DOWN and UP** strokes.

Notice how the strokes are played as you sing a particular word of the song. Sometimes you will use a down stroke quickly followed by and up stroke. Let's call this the '**DOWN/UP**' stroke (written as ⌐⌐ in the music).

The Wheels On The Bus

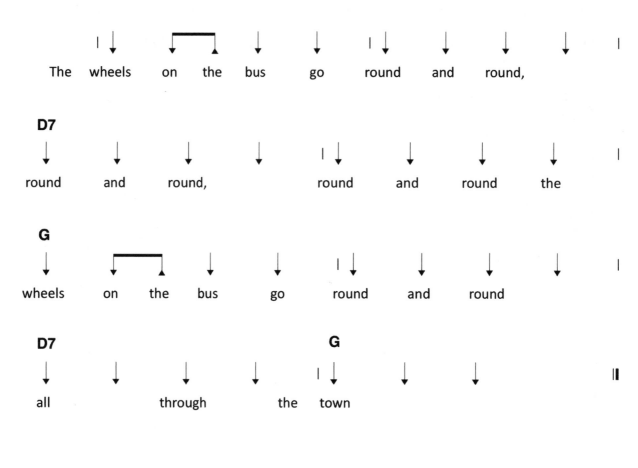

The   wheels   on   the   bus   go   round   and   round,

D7

round   and   round,   round   and   round   the

G

wheels   on   the   bus   go   round   and   round

D7   **G**

all   through   the   town

Now you can play the rest of the song using exactly the same strumming pattern. Here are the rest of the words. Don't forget to use your *DOWN/UP* stroke each time you sing '*on the*', and change chords where indicated:

2
G
The wipers *on the* bus go
Swish, swish, swish

D7
Swish, swish, swish
Swish, swish, swish

G
The wipers *on the* bus go
Swish, swish, swish

D7   **G**
All through the town

3
G
The horn *on the* bus goes
Beep, beep, beep

D7
Beep, beep, beep
Beep, beep, beep

G
The horn *on the* bus goes
Beep, beep, beep

D7   **G**
All through the town

4
G
The money *on the* bus goes
Clink, clink, clink

D7
Clink, clink, clink,
Clink, clink, clink.

G
The money *on the* bus goes,
Clink, clink, clink

D7   **G**
All through the town

5
G
The driver *on the* bus says
"Move on back

D7
move on back
move on back"

G
The driver *on the* bus says
"Move on back"

D7   **G**
All through the town

6
G
The people *on the* bus go
Up and down

D7
Up and down
Up and down

G
The people *on the* bus go
Up and down

D7   **G**
All through the town

7
G
The baby *on the* bus says
"Wah, wah, wah

D7
Wah, wah, wah
Wah, wah, wah"

G
The baby *on the* bus says
"Wah, wah, wah"

D7   **G**
All through the town

CHORD REMINDER!

G
X X 0 0 0 3

D7
X X 0 2 1 3

If You're Happy And You Know It

Let's try a new song, using **G**, **D7** and now **C** too.

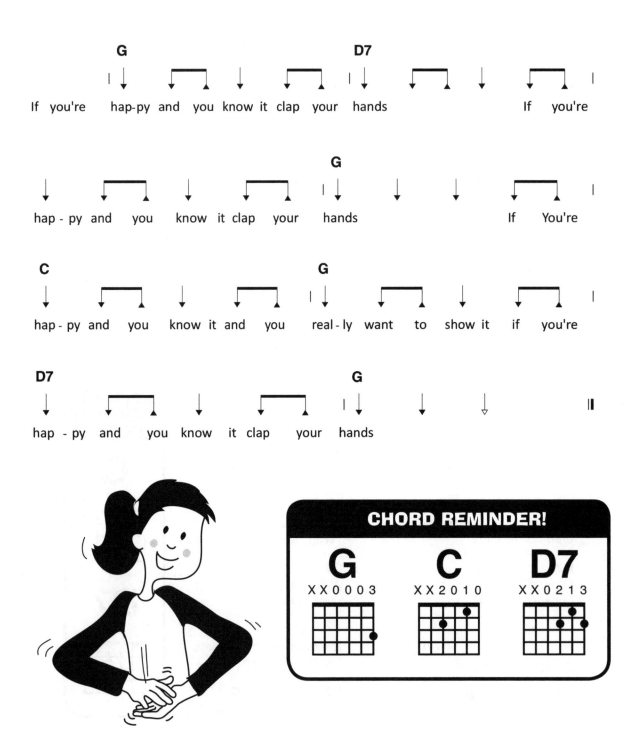

2   **G**
If you're happy and you know it

      D7
Stomp your feet (*stomp stomp*)

If you're happy and you know it

      G
Stomp your feet (*stomp stomp*)

    C
If you're happy and you know it

    G
And you really want to show it

   D7
If you're happy and you know it

    G
Stomp your feet (*stomp stomp*)

3   **G**
If you're happy and you know it

    D7
Shout "Hurray!" (*hoo-ray!*)

If you're happy and you know it

    G
Shout "Hurray!" (*hoo-ray!*)

    C
If you're happy and you know it

    G
And you really want to show it

   D7
If you're happy and you know it

    G
Shout "Hurray!" (*hoo-ray!*)

4   **G**
If you're happy and you know it

    D7
Do all three
(*clap-clap, stomp-stomp, hoo-ray!*)

If you're happy and you know it

    G
Do all three
(*clap-clap, stomp-stomp, hoo-ray!*)

    C
If you're happy and you know it

    G
And you really want to show it

   D7
If you're happy and you know it

    G
Do all three

Hooray!!

Old Macdonald Had A Farm

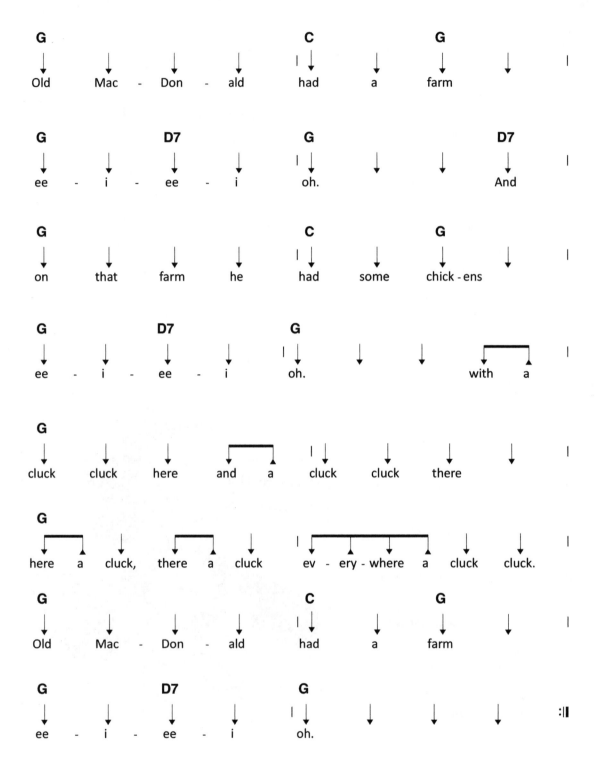

2 G   C   G   D7 G
Old MacDonald had a farm, ee i ee i oh

G   C   G   D7 G
And on that farm he had some dogs, ee i ee i oh

With a woof-woof here and a woof-woof there

Here a woof, there a woof, everywhere a woof-woof

              C   G   D7 G
Old MacDonald had a farm, ee i ee i oh

3 G   C   G   D7 G
Old MacDonald had a farm, ee i ee i oh

G   C   G   D7 G
And on that farm he had some turkeys, ee i ee i oh

With a gobble-gobble here and a gobble-gobble there

Here a gobble, there a gobble, everywhere a gobble-gobble

              C   G   D7 C
Old MacDonald had a farm, ee i ee i oh

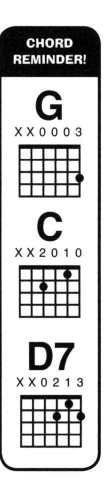

4 G   C   G   D7 G
Old MacDonald had a farm, ee i ee i oh

               C   G   D7 G
And on that farm he had some cows, ee i ee i oh

With a moo-moo here and a moo-moo there

Here a moo, there a moo, everywhere a moo-moo

              C   G   D7 G
Old MacDonald had a farm, ee i ee i oh

Baa Baa Black Sheep

G ↓ Baa ↓ baa ↓ black ↓ sheep **C** | ↓ have ↓ you ↓ a - ↓ ny **G** ↓ wool? ↓ |

C ↓ Yes ↓ sir, **G** ↓ yes ↓ sir, **D7** | ↓ three ↓ bags **G** ↓ full ↓ |

G ↓ one **C** ↓ for ↓ my ↓ mas - ↓ ter ↓ and **G** | ↓ one **D7** ↓ for ↓ my ↓ dame ↓ and |

G ↓ one **C** ↓ for ↓ the ↓ lit - ↓ tle ↓ boy ↓ who **D7** | ↓ lives ↓ down ↓ the **G** ↓ lane. ↓ :||

CHORD REMINDER!

G XX0003

C XX2010

D7 XX0213

Hickory Dickory Dock

G	D7	G			G	D7	G		
↓	↓	↓	↓	│↓		↓	↓	↓	│
Hickory	dickory	dock		the	mouse	ran up the	clock.		The

G	D7	C	G	D7		G		
↓	↓	↓	↓	│↓	↓	↓	↓	:‖
clock	struck	one, the	mouse ran	down		hickory	dickory	dock

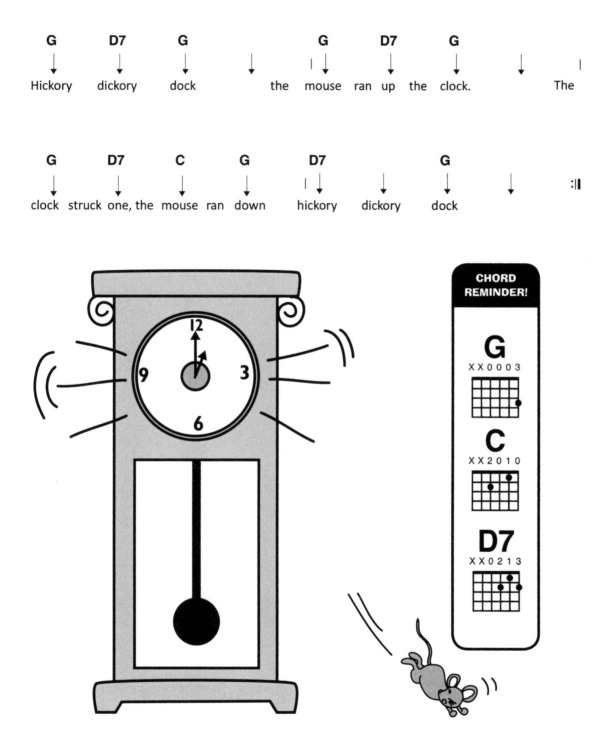

CHORD REMINDER!

G
XX0003

C
XX2010

D7
XX0213

Yankee Doodle

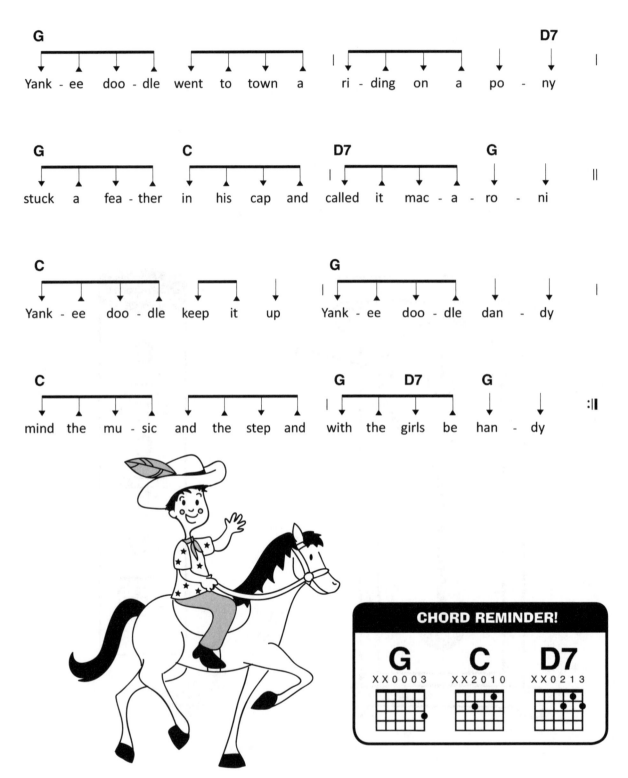

G											D7
↓	↓	↓	↓	↓	↓	↓	↓	↓	↓	↓	↓
Yank	- ee	doo	- dle	went	to	town	a	ri	- ding	on	a	po	- ny

G — Yank-ee doo-dle went to town a ri-ding on a po-ny |

G — stuck a fea-ther C — in his cap and D7 — called it mac-a-ro-ni G ||

C — Yank-ee doo-dle keep it up G — Yank-ee doo-dle dan-dy |

C — mind the mu-sic and the step and G — with the D7 — girls be G — han-dy :||

CHORD REMINDER!

G
XX0003

C
XX2010

D7
XX0213

Twinkle Twinkle Little Star

Oh Little Town Of Bethlehem

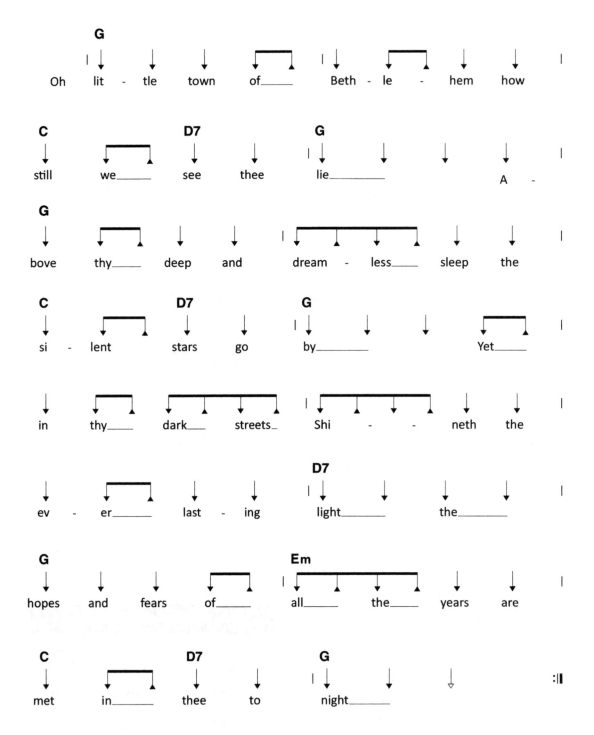

2

G
O morning stars, together

    C   D7 G
Proclaim the holy birth!

And praises sing to God the King

    C   D7 G
And peace to men on earth

For Christ is born of Mary

        D7
And gathered all above

    G   Em
While mortals sleep the Angels keep

    C   D7   G
Their watch of wondering love

3

G
How silently, how silently

    C   D7 G
The wondrous gift is given

So God imparts to human hearts

    C   D7 G
The blessings of His Heaven

No ear may hear His coming

        D7
But in this world of sin

    G   Em
Where meek souls will receive Him still

    C   D7   G
The dear Christ enters in

4

G
O holy Child of Bethlehem

    C   D7 G
Descend to us, we pray!

Cast out our sin and enter in

    C   D7 G
Be born in us to-day

We hear the Christmas angels

        D7
The great glad tidings tell

    G   Em
O come to us, abide with us

    C   D7 G
Our Lord Em-man-uel!

CHORD REMINDER!

G	C	D7	Em
XX0003	XX2010	XX0213	XX2000

Quiz: Name Parts of the Guitar

Fretboard

Headstock

Tuning Pegs

Bridge

Body

Strings

Nut

Frets

Soundhole

Neck

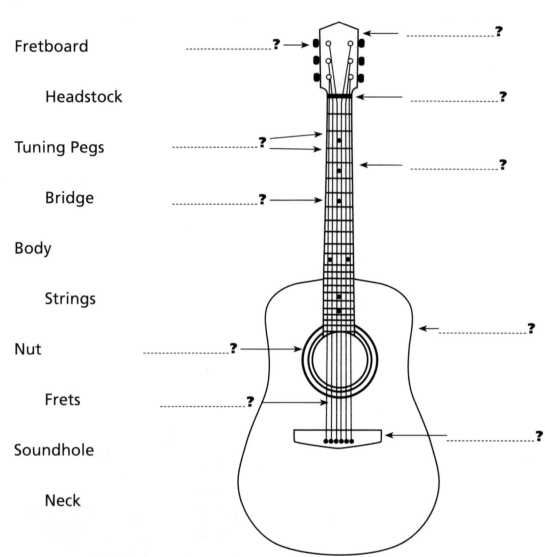

Quiz: Name That Chord

XX0213   XX2000   XX2010   XX0003

----------   ----------   ----------   ----------

MORE GREAT MUSIC BOOKS FROM KYLE CRAIG!

How To Play UKULELE — A Complete Guide for Absolute Beginners

978-1-908-707-08-6

My First UKULELE — Learn to Play: Kids

978-1-908-707-11-6

Easy UKULELE Tunes

978-1-908707-37-6

How To Play GUITAR — A Complete Guide for Absolute Beginners

978-1-908-707-09-3

My First GUITAR — Learn to Play: Kids

978-1-908-707-13-0

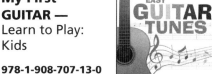

Easy GUITAR Tunes

978-1-908707-34-5

How To Play KEYBOARD — A Complete Guide for Absolute Beginners

978-1-908-707-14-7

My First KEYBOARD — Learn to Play: Kids

978-1-908-707-15-4

Easy KEYBOARD Tunes

978-1-908707-35-2

How To Play PIANO — A Complete Guide for Absolute Beginners

978-1-908-707-16-1

My First PIANO — Learn to Play: Kids

978-1-908-707-17-8

Easy PIANO Tunes

978-1-908707-33-8

How To Play HARMONICA — A Complete Guide for Absolute Beginners

978-1-908-707-28-4

My First RECORDER — Learn to Play: Kids

978-1-908-707-18-5

Easy RECORDER Tunes

978-1-908707-36-9

How To Play BANJO — A Complete Guide for Absolute Beginners

978-1-908-707-19-2

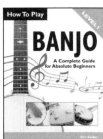

The GUITAR Chord Dictionary

978-1-908707-39-0

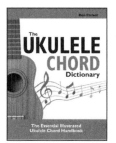

The UKULELE Chord Dictionary

978-1-908707-38-3